The Divine Eagle

Selwyn Hughes

© CWR 1988

**CWR, 10 Brooklands Close,
Sunbury-on-Thames, Middx TW16 7DX**

NATIONAL DISTRIBUTORS

Australia: Christian Marketing Pty Ltd., PO Box 154, North Geelong,
Victoria 3215   Tel: (052) 786100

Canada: Scripture in Song Recordings Ltd., PO Box 550, Virgil,
Ontario LOS 1TO   Tel: 416 641 0631

Malaysia: Salvation Book Centre, (M) Sdn. Bhd., 23 Jalan SS2/64,
47300 Petaling Jaya, Selangor

New Zealand: CWR (NZ), PO Box 4108, Mount Maunganui
Tel: (075) 57412

Singapore: Alby Commercial Enterprises Pte Ltd., Garden Hotel,
14 Balmoral Road, Singapore 1025

Southern Africa: CWR (Southern Africa), PO Box 2020, Clareinch, 7740 RSA
Tel: (021) 712560

Illustrations by Brian Norwood
Typeset by Watermark, Watford

Printed & bound in Great Britain

ISBN 1–85345–028–6 Hardback
ISBN 1–85345–029–4 Limp
First published 1981 and reprinted in illustrated format 1988

INTRODUCTION

Whilst most Christians know of God's promise of a fresh, new life, many have never experienced it for themselves. Their own spiritual lives never get off the ground.

The eagle teaches her young to fly by pushing them out of the nest ... and then swoops below, ready to catch them on her broad back. This may need to be repeated but soon the young eagle can fly. No longer falling and flapping but gliding and soaring as the thermal currents carry it upwards.

With clear teaching and insight, Selwyn Hughes shows how God is like a divine eagle who longs that we too might experience the exhilaration of soaring on wings like eagles.

THE DIVINE EAGLE ... TENDER AND LOVING

The idea for the theme The Divine Eagle arose out of
Deuteronomy 32:11 where God is pictured as a mother
Eagle pushing her offspring out of the nest in order to
teach them how to fly. Those who have studied the ways
of an eagle tell us she makes a wonderful mother. She
builds her nest in the tall trees away from the prying
hands of men, taking the utmost care to line it with the
softest feathers she can find. When her eggs hatch and

Deuteronomy
32:1–14

v.11

the little eaglets are born, she gives them her complete and undivided attention. Every morning she fills the nest with tasty morsels that will keep them going for the whole day. Nothing is too good for her precious brood.

After several weeks of this tender, loving care, the mother eagle suddenly changes in her behaviour. She knows it is now time for her eaglets to leave the nest and learn to fly. So, reaching down into the nest, she rips out the feathers, breaks up the twigs and overturns their nice, comfortable home. The little eaglets are frightened out of their wits. Gently she nudges one of the birds toward the edge of the overturned nest and pushes it out into the air. The little bird, of course, falls like a bullet to the ground, squawking with fright, but just as it is about to hit the ground, the mother eagle swoops beneath it, catches it on her broad wings and carries it safely up into the sky. Then she tilts her wing and the bird falls once again, but this time, as it flaps its wings in fright, it discovers it can fly! And this, my friend, is what God does with you and me. He pushes us out of our comfortable nests in order that we might expand our wings and soar toward His highest purposes.

Exodus 19:4
Deuteronomy 33:27

When once the mother eagle has taught the first of her eaglets to fly, she repeats the process with all the others until every one of her offspring are out of the nest and safely in the air. This gripping truth of God pushing us forward into greater usefulness – the Divine Eagle throwing us out of the nest to make us fly – is a divine principle that is deeply embedded in Scripture. If we fail to comprehend it, we deprive ourselves of an important spiritual insight.

We see it when we consider the captivity of the Children of Israel in Egypt. There can be no doubt that

Exodus 3:7–18

the Israelites were not greatly motivated to set out on the long march to the 'Promised Land' until God permitted Pharaoh to put such pressure upon them that they regarded any measures as better than their present distress. The oppression opened a door!

Our discomforts, sorrows, disappointments and overturned nests become what Howard Thurman calls 'the growing edge'. They become the starting points of progress. The deprivations we experience motivate us towards greater usefulness. How many of us would be where we are today had not God overturned our lives, changed our circumstances, allowed us to be disappointed and deprived, permitted us to walk

through the deepest darkness in order that we might find ourselves on 'the growing edge'. God had to upset us to set us up.

An illustration of this divine principle at work in the New Testament is seen when Jesus announced to His disciples that He was going away for good. The news must have hit them like a bombshell. Their hearts must have sunk within them with a strange sense of spiritual orphanage. They would be alone in this world without Him. They had banked everything on Jesus and, for His sake, they had left everything behind them – friends, families, everything. It was all an anti-climax, and worse – a collapse of all their hopes and

John 16:1–16

expectations. He said, in effect, 'My going is for your good. I will take away my presence but instead you will have my omnipresence. You will discover a new dimension in which I will be closer to you than I am at this moment. Now I am *with* you, but then I will be *in* you.' And isn't this precisely what happened? At Pentecost He came back – He did change His presence for His omnipresence. He came into the inner recesses of their hearts – burningly, blessedly near. They didn't simply remember Christ – they *realised* Him.

v. 7

Not only was His presence available, but His power was available – unlimited resources at their disposal at any and all times. When this happened, they knew He was right in taking away the comfort of His bodily presence to give them His spiritual presence – intimate, available and within. Mark this well: the Divine Eagle never disturbs our nest but for a good purpose and He never takes away the good without giving something much better.

We can learn to recognise specific events and occasions when God is likely to be implementing this principle in our lives. He does it, for example, when He overturns the nest of our calm and comfortable experiences and tips us out into the midst of fiery trials and tribulations. Have you gone through periods in your life when it seems that everything is running smoothly and you haven't a care in the world – then suddenly calamity strikes, and you find yourself saying, 'Just when everything seemed to be going fine – *this* had to happen.'

Many Christians, when faced with such a situation, think that sudden calamity or serious trouble is an indication that God is punishing them for some sin. This

attitude makes victory impossible. We must recognise, of course, that this is a world of moral consequences and that sin *does* bring trouble, but we are indebted to Jesus for showing us that sin and calamity are not always directly connected. In His comment on the fall of the

tower at Siloam and on those who lost their lives, Jesus said the sufferers were not worse sinners than the rest. Luke 13:4, 5

When trouble comes our attitude should be that described in James' letter, 'Greet it as pure joy, my brothers, when you encounter any sort of trial' (Moffatt). And why? Because what happens to us – sorrows, griefs, losses, disappointments – can help us to expand our wings and soar to new heights and new discoveries of God. Our inner attitudes determine the results.

James 1:1–16

Just in case anyone might misinterpret my meaning when I say that looking upon troubles as God's punishment for sin makes victory impossible, let me make it clear that I certainly believe *some* troubles are the direct result of personal sin. A lie, for example, can bring untold repercussions. Pre-marital sex can produce a pregnancy. When we violate God's laws then we have to suffer the consequences. The troubles I am talking about, however, are those which arrive upon our doorstep and for which we have no direct responsibility.

AN EAGLE SOARS

Isaiah says of the eagle that she 'soars' and not 'flaps'. Although, of course, an eagle is well able to use its wings to propel itself across the sky, its typical pose is that of soaring. An eagle will sometimes perch on a high rock and wait for a while – testing the winds. When it feels that the right wind is blowing, it expands its broad wings and is at once lifted by the breeze into the great heights. In every trial and difficulty that God allows to come our way, there is a breeze, that if we wait for it and take advantage of it, will lift us clean beyond the clouds where we will see the face of God. You see, life is determined more by our reactions than by our actions. When God allows things to crowd into your life, it is then that reaction counts. You can react in self-pity and in frustration or with confidence and courage and turn the trouble into a triumph.

Isaiah
40:25–31

v. 31

When trouble strikes and your nest is overturned – don't panic. Wait for the breeze that is springing up; it will lift you clean into the presence of God. Those that wait, that keep hoping, are those that soar. This is the eagle's secret of being able to soar so high – waiting. When troubles come, don't flap – soar!

If we are to live successfully as Christians we must come to grips with the fact that God does not permit trouble to come our way in order to destroy us but in order to develop us. When circumstances are against us, we must be able to set the tilt of our wings and use adversity to lift us higher into the presence of God.

When the storm strikes the eagle, if its wings are set in a downward tilt, it will be dashed to pieces on the ground; but if its wings are tilted upward, it will rise, making the storm bear it up beyond its fury. The Christian faith, providing we interpret it correctly and apply it to our circumstances, will set the wings of our spirit in the right direction, so that when trouble or calamity strikes, we go up and not down. The calamity that strikes one Christian finds him with his spiritual wings tilted in the direction of the earth so he writhes in anguish in the dust. The same calamity strikes another, one with his wings set upwards, and he soars above it – calm and serene.

Some students, discussing Romans 8:28, said to a professor in a theological college: 'But, professor, you don't believe that all things work together for good – all the pain, suffering and misery – do you?' The professor replied: 'The things, in themselves, may not be good, but God can make them work together for good.' That afternoon his wife was killed in an automobile accident. Before leaving the college, he dropped in to see the president and told him to give his students this message: 'Romans 8:28 still holds good.' When the professor died a year later, his friends and relatives inscribed Romans 8:28 on his tomb. Many a student has stood at that tomb and prayed that he might have that same spiritual insight. But it is not enough to have Romans 8:28 inscribed on our tomb, it must be inscribed in our life convictions.

Romans 8:28–39 v. 28

When we pursue the reasons why God overturns the nest of our calm and comfortable experiences and tips us out into the midst of seemingly endless difficulties and problems the clear conclusion is that He does it not in order to destroy us but to develop us. Hudson Taylor was seated in a room with a new missionary to China. He filled a glass with water, placed it on a table, and then

struck the table with his fist. As the water splashed out, he said to the young missionary: 'You will be struck by the blows of many sorrows and troubles in China, but remember, they will only splash out of you what is in you.' Out of some splash the emotions of bitterness, resentment and despair. Out of others splash joy, forgiveness and victory. Says Edwin Markham:

> Defeat may serve as well as victory
>   To shake the soul and let the glory out.
> When the great oak is straining in the wind
>   The boughs drink in new beauty, and the trunk
> Sends down a deeper root on the windward side.

An elderly Christian stood in the corridor of a train as it was coming into a station. The train lurched several times, before it stopped, throwing him from one side of the corridor to the other. When he hit one side, those near him heard him say, 'Hallelujah!' The jolting brought out what was in him. What does trouble do to you? Does it shake the glory out? If so, then you have victory!

Romans 8:14–27

WHAT LINES THE NEST?

Another nest that God often overturns in our lives is the
nest of *material prosperity*. This question of material Matthew
6:25–34
possessions is a sharp one. Some Christians prefer not to
face it as it raises all kinds of emotions in their hearts.
But, I assure you, if we don't face it, here and now, then
we leave God with no alternative but to deal firmly with
us. God will not have our heart fixed on *things*: He wants
our gaze fully focused on Himself. There is nothing v. 33
wrong with being the possessor of great riches,
providing these are held in trust for God and that we see
our role not as proprietors but as stewards of the Lord's
treasury. I have seen many Christians become
preoccupied with riches and I have watched with
interest as God overturned their nest.

A man I once knew, a Christian with a brilliant
business mind, launched an enterprise that, within a few
years, made him a fortune. When I talked to him about
his spiritual life, I was reminded once again of the words
of Edna St. Vincent Millay:

> *I cannot say what loves have come and gone.*
> *I only know that summer sang in me*
> *A little while, and in me sings no more.*

The icy winter of materialism had set in, chilling his
spiritual life. But then God overturned his nest. He was
stripped of everything he owned. At first he was stunned
and crushed. Out of the bewilderment and pain,
however, came a new vision of God. He rose up to build
a new and better business – one in which God was the
principal shareholder.

A Christian's relationship to material possessions is a vital issue. We read that 'Jesus sat down opposite the place where the offerings were put and watched ...' It is a solemn moment when we review our relationship to our money and material possessions with Him sitting beside us, watching the effect of money on us. The real question for us to ask, then, is this: Who owns my possessions, God or I? Whether we acknowledge it or

Mark 12:41–44

not, we do not in reality own anything. We are only in possession of our possessions for a brief period.

In the Bible God teaches us how to acknowledge His ownership – by giving Him one-tenth. But, remember, when we give one-tenth we are not really giving, we are only paying an obligation. When we give out of the remaining nine-tenths, only then are we giving. A Christian businessman put it wisely when he said, 'God has prospered me. Now I want to know how much of God's money I can keep for my own needs.'

Unless we develop the right attitude towards our money and our material possessions then God may have

to overturn our nest in order for us to learn the lesson that our gaze must be focused on God – not gold. When we learn to put all our possessions at God's disposal, we do more than settle a money issue – we settle a life attitude. We then become men and women under orders, people with a sense of mission, a sense of direction and goal.

1 Timothy 6:7–16

When you let go of your possessions and let God have them then life takes on a sense of stewardship. You are handling something on behalf of Another. That does something to the whole of life – puts sacredness into the secular and lifts the sordid into the sacred. Surrender of

your possessions to God makes them sanctified and sanctifying. Your Christianity functions in and through the material.

Many years ago I heard an old Welsh preacher begin a sermon with these words, 'Tonight I want to speak to you on the subject: "What Jesus talked about most".' Luke 12:13–21 Immediately my mind jumped ahead of him and I tried to work out for myself just what it was that Jesus talked about most. I thought to myself, could it be 'prayer' or 'faith' or 'heaven'? No, I concluded, it was none of these. It must be *this* – 'Salvation'. Imagine my surprise when the preacher said, 'The subject Jesus talked about most v. 15 was a man's relationship to his possessions.' Consider the facts for yourself. Half of Jesus' parables focus on the issue of money. In Matthew's gospel alone Jesus talks about money close on 100 times. In fact, extending the argument further than the gospels, although in the New Testament there are about 500 references to prayer, there are over 1,000 references to a person's relationship to his possessions. I believe that God calls some people to go into business as definitely as He calls some to go into the ministry of the Church. There they can use their powers of organisation and administration to make money for Romans 12:1–18 God. Someone asked Jane Addams, the founder of many homes for waifs and strays, what it was that made her go into this kind of work. She replied, 'I looked into the faces of the ruffian kids and then I looked into the face of Christ, and I gave my life to business to help meet that need.' I can imagine a Christian businessman or businesswoman saying, 'I looked into the faces of the poor and needy in this world and then I looked into the v. 8 face of Christ, and gave my life to business to meet that need.'

A businessman or businesswoman whose life is dedicated to God will go about their tasks with a lightness of step, a sureness of direction and a sense of mission. They are making money for God.

Livingstone's motto should become the motto of

every Christian in the world. Repeat it to yourself slowly through the day: 'I will place no value on anything that I have or possess except in relation to the Kingdom of Christ.' If it furthers the Kingdom: it has value, it can stay. If it is useless to the Kingdom – it must go.

Unless we have this issue straight then we may soon find our nest overturned. I say again, God will not have our gaze focused on *things* but only on Himself. When once the central issue of who owns our possessions is fixed – God and not ourselves – we are then free to cultivate generosity. We must decide that our outlook on everything and everybody should be to find the good, further the good and do good in every situation. Someone has said, 'If we do not give according to our resources then God will make our resources according to our giving.' Does this make God a tyrant? Not if we understand things correctly, for the more we give to others, the more beautiful we become in ourselves. The giving are the living – in themselves!

Matthew 6:19–24

Matthew 6:22 says that if our eye, our outlook on life, our whole way of looking at things and people, is good, or generous, then our whole personality is illuminated. We become better by our giving. A rich Christian businessman who decided to donate some important medical equipment to a hospital in China, went to see the ship on which the equipment was being carried. At the dockside he met another Christian and as they talked, the businessman shared with him what the moment meant to him. 'I, too, have a gift on board that ship,' said the other Christian. 'My only daughter is on board, going to China as a missionary.' The businessman said, 'My brother, my sacrifice is nothing compared to what you have given.' Both, however, were

v. 22

stewards of the entrustments of God. Both could say, 'Such as I have, I give.'

In this parable Jesus mentions two things that choked the growing wheat and made it unfruitful: 'As for him who is sown "among thorns," that is the man who listens

Matthew 13:1–23

to the word, but the worry of the world and the delight v. 22
of being rich choke the word; so it proves unfruitful'
(Moffatt). Here 'worry' and 'the delight of being rich' are
classed as the two outstanding enemies of growth. Now
note that Jesus didn't say that riches were the enemy of
the soul but 'delight of being rich', that is, wealth as an
end in itself. Someone has said, 'You can serve God with
mammon but you can't serve God and mammon.'

'Is not life more than meat?' asks Jesus. 'No,' say many Matthew 6:25
of the modern men and women of this generation. 'Life
is food,' says the biochemist. 'You are what you eat.'
'Life is emotion,' says the sensualist. 'You are what you
experience in your emotions.' 'Life is possessions,' says
the materialist. 'You are what you own.' But the
Christian says, 'Life is Christ. He is supreme. He
controls the food, the emotions and the money.' They
are servants of a divine purpose, hence purified and
redeemed. Without that purpose, the purification turns
into putrefaction. 'Whoever craves wealth for its own
sake,' says a Welsh proverb, 'is like a man who drinks sea
water; the more he drinks the more he thirsts, and he
ceases not to drink until he perishes.'

THE DIVINE EAGLE – ABUNDANT LIFE

Another nest which God seeks to overturn in our lives is the nest of *spiritual complacency*. Many Christians are content to snuggle down in their spiritual nest and live out their Christian lives at a level far below the best. It might be warm and comfortable in the nest, but it is better by far to expand one's wings, launch out into the clear, blue sky and live life to its fullest potential. Mark this and mark it well – God's desire is to get you out of the nest and up into the air. I am thinking particularly at this moment, however, of those Christians who, although soundly saved and fully committed to Jesus Christ, have never experienced all the fullness of the Holy Spirit. You see, although every Christian has the Holy Spirit, the Holy Spirit does not have every Christian. When you surrendered your life to Jesus Christ, the Holy Spirit came in to regenerate you, give you a new birth, but now you need to experience another encounter with the Spirit that lifts you clean out of the nest and up into the air.

1 Corinthians 12:3

The Good Shepherd came not merely to give us life but to give it – *abundantly*. One writer says of this verse: 'At conversion, Christ gives us life, but when we experience the fullness of the Spirit, we encounter not merely life, but life that is abundant. In conversion, God's life is imparted to us. In the fullness of the Spirit, God's life inundates us.'

John 10:1–10

v. 10

It is the margin between life and life abundant that measures the difference between muddling through this business of living and living with spiritual poise and power. Many of us are living too close to our margins. We are like the little girl who, when asked how she came to fall out of bed, replied, 'I slept too close to the place where I got in.' Despite the fact that we are living in what some call 'The Charismatic Age', there are still multitudes of Christians who lack a vital encounter with the Holy Spirit. Ask yourself: Is my relationship with the Holy Spirit one merely of belief or one of experience?

Ephesians 5:18

Many believe in the Spirit but they have never fully surrendered to Him; they are still in the nest when they ought to be up in the air. Rufus Jones remarks that by the time the creeds were written, all the Church could say was, 'I believe in the Holy Spirit.' At great length the Church outlined the facts of the life of Jesus – the Incarnation, Crucifixion, Resurrection, Ascension – but the Holy Spirit was mentioned as a belief, a belief instead of an experience. Here is where the faith of many present-day Christians is in need of a boost.

THE EAGLE AND THE SPIRIT

The question must now be faced: Must we, in seeking the fullness of the Spirit, face another crisis similar to conversion? Yes, I think that usually we must. I would not lay it down as an infallible rule because some people have such a dramatic conversion that they seem to appropriate all God has for them from the word 'Go'. Most of us, however, would share the experience of a great 'Holiness' preacher of a past generation, who said 'The soul gets by on a series of crises.'

The spiritual movements that are making the greatest headway in today's Church all converge on one fact – the necessity of bringing the whole life into line with the will of God. There must be an absoluteness about the whole thing. And they would agree that while conversion begins this process, a further crisis, in some form or another, is necessary to bring everything into line. Are they all wrong about this? I think not. They may be wrong in certain emphases or certain claims, but in the one central thing, I believe they are profoundly right. In my own life and in the lives of thousands of others with whom I have dealt intimately, I have seen the principle at work, that when we come to the end of our own strength, we can either sink back and become a mediocre Christian or give ourselves in total abandonment to the person of the Holy Spirit, for Him to empower us, enlighten us and energise us. Permit me to ask you a very personal question: Are you living a Spirit-filled life? Are you conscious of His residency and presidency in your heart? If not, you are still in the nest. It's time you got up into the air.

The Christian faith is a religion of the Spirit. Jesus was

Romans 8:2

conceived by the Spirit, the Spirit descended upon Him at His baptism, He was led by the Spirit into the wilderness, He came out in the power of the Spirit, began His ministry by saying, 'The Spirit of the Lord is upon me,' cast out evil spirits by the Spirit of God, was offered up as a sacrifice through the eternal Spirit, was raised from the dead by the Spirit of holiness, issues commandments by the Spirit and baptises in the Spirit. As His followers, we are led by the Spirit, made into Christ's image by the Spirit, we bring forth the fruit of the Spirit, our mortal bodies are quickened by the Spirit and 'the law of the Spirit of life in Christ Jesus' delivers us from 'the law of sin and death'. From first to last the Christian faith is a religion of the Spirit.

It is a religion of the Spirit conditioned by the content Jesus puts within it by His life and teaching. Just as Jesus reveals the nature of the Father so He reveals the nature Matthew 3:11 of the Spirit. If God is a Christlike God then the Spirit is a Christlike Spirit. This is very important because men have made the Holy Spirit appear strange and even bizarre. A man told me once that the Spirit had told him to take two wives – one to meet his physical needs and the other to meet his spiritual needs. When I suggested to him that the Spirit would never tell him to do anything that contradicted the character of Jesus, he told me he was led by the Spirit not by Jesus. If we are truly led by the Spirit then we will become more and more like Jesus or it won't be the Holy Spirit that is leading us but some other spirit.

The nature and operation of the Holy Spirit prior to the coming of Jesus is somewhat difficult to understand. In the Old Testament, for example, the Spirit appears to have no permanent abiding place on the earth. He comes and goes, alights upon men for a specific task, then returns to heaven. On some occasions the Spirit used men whose lives quite clearly lacked dedication and holiness. All this could lead to wrong conclusions about the Spirit. This is why God gave the Spirit sparingly to

men until Jesus came and fixed the content of the Spirit. It is only in Jesus that we see the full and final revelation of the Spirit's work and purpose in the world.

What does the life and teaching of Jesus reveal about the character and content of the Spirit? Two things – He is the Spirit of power and the Spirit of purity. When Jesus was about to return to heaven, He promised His Acts 1:1–12 disciples that if they would tarry in Jerusalem for the 'promise of the Father', they would receive supernatural v. 8 power that would transform them from being weak, timid, vacillating disciples into men ablaze and invincible. Did this happen? It most certainly did. In the Upper Room the disciples received such an invasion of power, it completely revolutionised their personalities.

The fullness of the Spirit means that we avail ourselves not only of His power but also of His purity. Here the Christian Church tends to become unbalanced. Some parts of the Church place the emphasis on the obtaining of spiritual power and claim that what we need is more of God's supernatural gifts such as prophecy, the word of knowledge, working of miracles and so on. Another section of the Church says, 'No, this is not our greatest need. What we need,' they claim, 'is to seek God for more holiness and greater purity.' Both are right, of course, and yet both are wrong. It is a common temptation in Christian circles to alight upon one aspect of truth, hold it up for attention and say, 'This is where our gaze must be focused.' This is how denominations began – by the emphasis of one aspect of truth to the exclusion of others.

Let's be quite clear about this. If we are to become like Jesus then we need both qualities – purity *and* power. Galatians 5:16– When we examine the Acts of the Apostles, we find that the coming of the Holy Spirit brought both purity and power into the hearts of those early Christians. The fact that they were empowered is seen quite clearly from the evidence in the Upper Room. The timid, frightened disciples became as bold as lions when once the Spirit came upon them. The fact that they were purified is also quite clearly seen, for when Peter interprets the coming of the Spirit upon the Gentiles, he says, 'He made no distinction between them, but purified their hearts by faith'. Cleansing of the heart came as a result of the coming of the Spirit.

Acts 15:9

SOAR TO ... CREATIVE LIVING

Another reason why God gently nudges us out of our nest is to enable us to experience what Paul Tournier calls 'the adventure of living'. I am convinced that the vast majority of us are content to settle for the accustomed rather than the adventurous. We take the little and we lose the big. God has designed us for creative living, creative thinking and creative venture. We are only truly fulfilled when we live, think and act creatively. Some of you, whose lives are rather humdrum, may be saying to yourselves at this moment, 'Well, that lets me off the hook. Creative thinking is for others with more education and more potential than I have to offer.' But you are quite wrong. God wants *you* to live creatively, and He comes to you now, through these words, in order to give you a gentle push out of the nest.

Some years ago a famous hotel in California, the El Cortez Hotel, had a serious problem. Its one elevator could not cope with the needs of the guests. The management decided to call in some architects who suggested that another elevator should be installed. To do this, they said, a hole would have to be made from the basement to the roof, and would involve putting the hotel out of service for a whole season. A cleaner, overhearing the discussions, said, 'Why don't you build it on the outside?' Astonished, the architects looked at each other. Then someone said, 'Why not?' El Cortez Hotel became the first building in history to have an elevator built on the outside. Although all human beings have a capacity to be creative, only a Christian who is wholly dedicated to God has the potential for a fully dynamic and adventurous life.

One of the greatest mistakes we can make in life is to block the efforts of the Divine Eagle when He attempts to push us out of the nest of the accustomed into the world of the adventurous. Asher did this – the account in the *Moffat* translation reads: 'Asher sat still by the sea board clinging to his creeks.' Although the metaphor is now changed from a 'nest' to a 'creek', the principle is still the same. There was Asher sitting by the seaboard, clinging to his creeks, when he could have launched out into the ocean and experienced the joy of a great adventure. In the face of the big, he settled for the little. They were 'his' creeks and he wasn't going to let the accustomed go to venture into the unaccustomed no matter how great the possibilities.

Judges 5:13–18

v. 17

Asher is a type of the Christian who wants to stay by the safe and secure, and finishes up by doing nothing and getting nowhere. Now don't misunderstand what I am saying here. I am not advocating spiritual recklessness nor am I arguing for an unmindful approach to the Christian life, I am simply saying that we ought to be ocean-minded and not creek-minded Christians. The people who try to find poise and inner security by clinging to the creeks are invariably unfulfilled for we are inwardly made for growth and creativity. Changing the metaphor once again, someone has said that a turtle doesn't get anywhere until he sticks his neck out! To cling to our creeks for safety and security is to be upset at every call of the big. We are made for the big and are restless in our littleness. We cannot be content this side of God's purpose.

Meditating on the issue of the Divine Eagle pushing us out of the nest of the accustomed in order that we might experience the adventurous, we ask ourselves a question: How does God go about doing this? He does it first by dropping a powerful thought or idea into our minds. Today as you go about your daily tasks, hundreds of thoughts will flow through your mind. Many of them will arise from your subconscious. Some will come from Satan. Others will come from God. The thoughts that

come from God are sometimes so challenging that we ignore them and push them right out of our minds.

'It is the glory of God to conceal a matter; to search out a matter is the glory of kings.' God carefully, quietly hides His most precious gifts so that we may become joyous 'kings' by discovering them. It is a universal truth that the most valuable treasures are hidden from clear view. The pearl is hidden within the oyster. The diamond is buried deep within the earth. The gold nugget is concealed in the heart of a great mountain. God plans life in such a way that the greatest treasures are

Proverbs 25:2

concealed, waiting for you to discover them. And there is no thrill like the thrill of making a great discovery. You will feel like a king.

Today you must begin to discover the treasures that God has hidden within your thoughts. Be on the look-out for God's 'deposits' in your mind. An idea will come to you and at first you will say, 'Go away, go away,' but learn to ask yourself: 'Is this what God is saying to me?' Don't push a thought away because it is too challenging. Welcome it. This doesn't mean that every big and great idea must be acted upon. It has to be

considered, weighed, evaluated and analysed to see whether it has really come from God. Take more time in looking at your thoughts. Perhaps while you are reading these lines, God will drop an idea into your mind that will transform your relationships, your service or your vocation.

We can see that adventurous living begins when we allow God to push us out of the nest into more creative ways of thinking and living. We often speak of the hardening of the arteries as one of the dangers of our advancing years, but as Dr Douglas Speere says, 'Our greatest danger is not hardening of the arteries but hardening of the attitudes.' We harden our viewpoint, refuse to look at anything beyond that viewpoint. We groove our thinking and acting, and the grooves get deeper and deeper until they become graves that bury us. As someone put it, 'You don't grow old; you get old by not growing.' Some people are dead at 40, although their funerals are postponed until they are 60. For many Christians, life has settled into ruts – mental, physical and spiritual ruts. 'And a rut,' said someone, 'is a grave with both ends knocked out.'

In Canada I saw a dirt road leading off the main highway which had a sign on it that read, 'Choose your rut – you will be in it for the next 20 miles.' When New Year's Day comes, many could say to themselves: 'I'd better choose my rut, for I'll be in it for the next 365 days.' Life for them is not an adventure. It holds no surprises, offers no excitement and is uncreative. My friend, I beg you, open your mind to God today and don't resist the Divine Eagle as He prepares to push you out into a more creative way of thinking, acting and living. Someone has said that the last words of the Church

when it is taken up to heaven will be these: 'It has never been done like this before.' Focus your mind on Psalm 104, and keep in mind that the God who created all things desires to live, move and think in you.

Psalm 104

Dr Halford Luccock in his book, *Marching off the Map*, quotes Gibbon's indictment of the monks of Constantinople, the sterile pedants of the 10th century: 'They held in their lifeless hands the riches of their fathers, without inheriting the spirit which had created that sacred patrimony. They read, they praised, they compiled; but their languid souls seemed alike incapable of action and thought.' If Jesus were here today He would probably say: 'Beware of the monks of Constantinople.' If Jesus were to look into our eyes today, would He read there the same sterility?

We are in one of the most exciting decades of history. It is true there are great problems, but there are also great possibilities. Science continues to make great strides, crossing frontiers hitherto undreamed of, and showing a quality of thinking that is utterly breathtaking. And what of the Christian Church in such an era? We are, generally speaking, like those of whom Coleridge speaks: 'People with bedridden truths which lie asleep in the dormitory of their minds.' Many of us hold truths, but they are bedridden truths – they don't walk and dance and go in procession, with banners waving. I am not referring, of course, to the timeless, changeless truths of the Incarnation, Redemption, etc., but the truths of translating the Gospel message in terms that really communicate to the men and women of this age. How tragic that so many of us are asleep when the world is awake – bedfast when the world is on the march.

Ephesians
3:7–21

v. 7

SOAR ... TO CHANGE

To break the stalemate in our lives and begin to think and act creatively. We must first, *recognise that although the body is doomed to decay, this is not so with the mind.* Your mind and thoughts are capable of infinite growth and development. Right up to the moment you die, your thoughts can be alert and growing.

Philippians 2:1–11

Second, *don't keep looking back at past achievements, look forward to the future accomplishments.* Jesus said, 'No man ... looking back is fit for the kingdom.' He cannot fit into the Kingdom for the Kingdom is ongoing, outreaching, creative, redemptive.

Luke 9:62

Third, *break up the old patterns of thought every day by doing something you have never done before.* If you follow a consistent route on your way to work, take another one. If you have regular meals, do without one to show you can. Break up routines now and again, for routines can become ruts.

Fourth, *keep a mental and spiritual wastebasket so that you can discard old ideas.* Throw away the bad to get the good, throw away the good to get the better, throw away the better to get the best. A head of a school said, pointing to an incinerator, 'Without this the school couldn't keep going.' Get rid of old ideas to make way for better ones.

Fifth, *let Christ stimulate your mind into greater creativity.* In Christ you have the most absolutely stimulating force in the universe. He coaxes a summer out of a winter, a bird out of a shell and life out of a dead spirit. Expose your whole being to His stimulus and be the person He designed you to be.

SOAR TO ... SELF-ACCEPTANCE

Another reason why the Divine Eagle gently nudges us out of the nest is in order that we might learn *to become totally honest and authentic human beings*. What do I mean? Many of us, because we don't know how to face the fears, the guilts, the inferiority feelings and the hurts within us, push those things deep down into our personalities and go about pretending they are not there. Rather than expose a self, either to ourselves or others, which we imagine to be ugly or inadequate, we instinctively wear a mask and pretend to be someone we are not. While it might seem to be a safer life behind this mask, it is also a lonely life. We cease to be authentic, and as persons we cease to grow. We are simply not being ourselves, and when the curtain drops after our performance, we remain the same, immature persons that we were when the curtain went up at the beginning of our act.

Psalm 51:1–17

I know that for many the reality of facing themselves as they are, and accepting themselves as they are, is a challenge from which they would shrink. If you feel this way now don't, I beg you, resist the nudge of the Divine Eagle as He gently pushes you toward the edge of the nest. If you let God have His way in your heart and life, a new dimension of living can open up for you.

The mask that so many of us wear says, 'I am not sure you would like me as I am, so I will present myself the way I would like you to see me.' And that, deep down, is dishonesty.

Someone might say, 'But how can we accept ourselves, our faults, our failures, our mistakes, our blunders and our inadequacies, until we have reached

spiritual maturity?' Accepting ourselves as we are does not mean that we will not dislike our failures, our mistakes and our inadequacies. It means that we will not be bowled over by them or intimidated by them to the extent that we lose our spiritual balance. Whenever we make a mistake, commit a sin or make a foolish blunder,

Hebrews
12:1–13
v. 6

God begins to work in our lives to correct the situation. But His corrections and His disciplines are always motivated by love and compassion. He is never punitive, judgemental or authoritarian. And the way God deals with us is the way we must deal with ourselves.

Permit me to share with you how the truth of self-acceptance has worked in my own life. Ever since I can remember I have always been an idealist, wanting to resolve all my personal problems and hang-ups so that I could get on with the business of living and teaching others how to live. At times I have been intensely angry at my own immaturity. I wanted to grow up quickly, find

the answers to all of my questions, resolve all my inner conflicts and present myself to the Church as 'Mr Perfect'. The gap between what I was and what I felt I ought to be was something I struggled to close. So much so, that in one period of my life I became greatly disillusioned and dejected. I was being harder on myself than God was, and my own punitive and harsh self-judgments worked to compound the problem rather than resolve it.

Mark 12:31

It was in the midst of this predicament that God revealed Himself to me and showed me that He accepted me as I was – faults, failures, mistakes, misunderstand-

ings notwithstanding – and that the gap between what I was and what I knew I ought to be could only be closed by resting in His love rather than by frantic struggle and inward striving. God enabled me to accept myself and to live with myself in the knowledge that day by day the gap would close, and that I would grow toward the goal that He has set for my life. I have learned to accept myself as God accepts me, and to discipline myself as God disciplines me – in love. The pressure to grow is no longer a harsh one. I am learning to love myself as God loves me.

Each one of us tends to evaluate ourselves the way our parents evaluated us. If, for example, we had parents who acted harshly toward us whenever we made a mistake, became extremely punitive and judgemental in their attitudes, then we tend to apply those same standards toward ourselves in our adult years.

Some parents, whenever their children make a mistake, come down upon them heavily and use such words as 'stupid', 'idiot', 'lazy', 'fool' – and so on. These words, linked together with stern, disapproving attitudes, if given consistently through the developmental years, greatly affect a child's self-understanding so that when they arrive in adult life, the evaluative part of their personality is set. It is not a universal principle, of course, because some people brought up in an environment such as I have described, break away from such negative influences and develop a healthy self-concept. This, however, is more the exception than the rule.

If we are to accept ourselves as we are, we must look at the way God views us. Whenever we make a mistake, commit a sin or err in some way, God begins to discipline us. But it must be noted, His discipline is never given in anger but always in love. He corrects us not because He delights to punish us, but because He loves us too much to let us get away with things that will hinder our spiritual growth and maturity. And that, I say again, is the same attitude we must show toward ourselves.

Colossians 1:9–14

SOAR TO ... THE CHALLENGE OF CONVERSION

That many of the attitudes we have toward ourselves are
hangovers from our past relationships brings up the
question: Doesn't conversion eliminate these difficulties
and give us new understanding and enlightenment? Not
always. Conversion must not be viewed as a cure-all for
our problems. This is not to devalue conversion but to
understand it. Conversion sometimes intensifies our
problems because it forces issues to the surface in our
lives which we are obliged to deal with if we are to move
on to spiritual maturity.

What, then, does conversion mean? It means we have
started but not finished. If, for example, someone grows
up experiencing little love, affection or kindness, there
are problems created in that person's life which
conversion does not always cure. God comes in at
conversion to help that person work through those
problems, and such is the miracle of His presence, that
the very deprivation becomes an opportunity to
experience more of God's power and love than would
otherwise be possible. The groaning point, hurt and
deprivation, now becomes the growing point to a greater
awareness of God and the reality of His love. Maturity
doesn't mean having all my problems solved, but
learning to accept myself and live with myself,
recognising all the time that God is quietly nurturing
me, developing me and changing me into His image.
What a freedom this brings into the personality. A man
in a group with whom I once shared this truth said, 'The
thing that scares me about removing my mask is finding
that you won't love me as I am.' I asked him if he loved
himself in the true Biblical sense of that phrase and he

Colossians
1:28–2:10

admitted he didn't. When he worked on this problem and came to accept himself, he was then able to remove his mask and say, 'This is what I'm really like. You may or may not like me as I am but this is all I've got. God loves me and I love myself, so even if you don't love me,

it is better for me and you that I am honest, for in honesty and openness lie a power that makes for my positive development and growth.'

Removing our mask is risky, but it is equally risky not to remove it. To keep trying to be what others expect us to be or want us to be, without ever coming to any real self-understanding, leads not to growth but to spiritual immaturity. The truth is, the harder we try to please everyone, the more certain it is that we will please no one. You must be yourself – in Christ. The question may be asked: Does this mean that I must now go about shocking people into reality by saying, 'Look, this is what I am really like. How do you like the real *me?*'

Dr Paul Tournier was once asked at a conference just how much openness one should practice with others. He replied, 'Be prepared to say it all, but say only what you feel God is leading you to say.' Wise advice. Being prepared to say it all relieves us of our fear of exposing ourselves or being exposed, so that we can respond to another in loving honesty without the fear of saying too much. In being free to say it all, we are also free to be silent when we should be. So often we want to share our strengths but not our weaknesses.

2 Corinthians 12:1–10

Some time ago in a counselling session, a woman shared with me about a matter that brought her great discouragement. It so happened that something similar had happened to me around the same time, and I took the opportunity to share with her my discouragement. She was overcome and said, 'I never thought you could be discouraged.' Later she said that my frankness brought her great hope, and out of it God ministered to her need. Christ ministered to this woman out of my weakness not out of my strength!

v. 9

SOAR TO ... TRIUMPHANT FAITH

We move now to yet another aspect of the Divine Eagle – and we focus on the issue of how God sometimes overturns the nest *of an uncertain and troubled faith* in order that we might come to know the joy of a serene and triumphant faith. Let me clarify what I mean. There are a great many who have a faith in God, but it isn't an adequate, working faith. It doesn't function at the place of poise and power. The headmaster of a school in India was invited to attend a Christian gathering where it was announced that a famous missionary would answer questions on matters relating to the Christian faith. The headmaster declined to attend, giving this as his reason: 'At the moment I have a satisfactory faith but if I come to that meeting, a non-Christian might ask a question which will upset my faith.' His faith was a troubled one – not a triumphant one.

How does God go about the task of helping us attain a serene, assured faith rather than one that is uncertain and inadequate? Does He keep dark and desolating doubts from us? Does He protect us from the incisive questions of non-believers? No. He gently nudges us out of the nest, forces us to face the reality of a world where our faith is put to the test, makes sure that we come face to face with issues that have to be grappled with, for He knows that it is by grappling that we grow. Someone has said, 'The Church is no candle – blow on.' He was referring to the fact that the Church is indestructible. But the same can be said of the Christian faith. We can face all the doubts and questions people throw at us. The Christian faith 'is no candle – blow on'.

1 Peter 1:23

There are two major approaches to life, the Christian approach and the scientific approach. The Christian approach works from facts up to conclusions. Both come out at the same place – they say the same thing. Not one single fact has been discovered in the heavens above, or in the earth beneath, to invalidate a single thing as it is contained in the Christian faith that centres in Jesus. The discoveries of science have done nothing but corroborate Him, for His laws are written into the very nature of reality. All that science does is uncover those laws. The God of nature and the God of the Bible are not two different gods – they are one God, and that one God is the Father of our Lord Jesus Christ. The laws of the universe, the laws of our relationships, the laws of our physical bodies, the laws of our minds are turning out to be the laws of Christ. They fit.

Colossians
1:15–23

v. 16

We must work our way through this scientific climate, and hopefully come out not simply with a faith that we sustain but with a faith that sustains us. We must not be afraid of the 20th century with its great scientific advances, its space shuttles, its nuclear energy and its amazing discoveries. Neither must we shrink from facing fearlessly the challenge this age brings us in terms of our faith.

We must ask ourselves the intriguing question: Can we take the same steps in verifying the Christian faith as science takes in verifying its knowledge of things that can be weighed and measured? I believe we can. There

are five steps in the scientific method: (1) The statement of the problem. (2) The selection of a hypothesis to meet the problem. (3) Experimentation with the hypothesis. (4) Verifying the hypothesis on a wide scale. (5) A simple and humble sharing of the verified results.

Let us take this five-fold method and apply it to the realm of the spiritual. First – *the statement of the problem.* The problem is how to develop a serene and joyous faith in the midst of a world beset by so many difficulties. Next comes *the selection of a hypothesis to meet the problem.* Let your mind sweep the horizon of possibilities as to who best illustrates a serene and

joyous faith, and who do you come up with? Christ. We have but to turn to the account of His life to find it so. Every line speaks of poise and every line speaks of power. And yet the poise and power were manifested in the midst of great problems and difficulties. He went into the wilderness for 40 days and was tempted by the devil there. We would expect to see Him emerge from that shattered and exhausted. On the contrary, the account says that He 'returned in the power of the Spirit'. That which was intended to weaken Him ended only by strengthening Him. Here is the authentic attitude we are looking for – an attitude that uses everything, transforms everything and grows by grappling with difficulties, not withdrawing from them.

Luke 4:1–14

v. 14

Next we come to the third step in the scientific verification – *experimentation with the hypothesis.* Someone might ask: Isn't Christ's faith something that is unique, incapable of being duplicated? An examination of the New Testament shows that not only did Jesus possess a serene and joyous faith in the midst of great and stupendous difficulties, but He seemed to be able to pass on to those who were His followers the same spirit of victory over all things. In living fellowship with Him, His disciples had the very same serenity and poise. If this was not true then Christ's movement would now be a monument, instead of a living organism that has spread across the face of the earth. We have only to link ourselves with Jesus Christ, live in daily fellowship with Him, draw from His unending supplies, and His faith becomes our faith. I used to be the most negative person in the little Welsh village where I lived until I met Jesus Christ. Instantly my life changed. Where before I withdrew from life, I found I wanted to face everything.

Acts 4:1–13

All my 'No's' turned to 'Yes's'. I stopped having conferences with fear and instead I had them with faith. It was Jesus who made the difference.   v. 13

The fourth step of scientific verification is *verifying the hypothesis on a wide scale*. In the Christian Church we have the world's greatest collective verification. It stretches into all countries, all races and colours and all cultures. Although separated by different languages, the   Revelation 7:9–17

members of Christ's Body unite to speak a common language – the language of a tried and proven faith. It is the language of an experience of God in Christ. That language is the language of certainty. The accents differ, the language is the same. I have heard this language in every part of the world as I have travelled around. It is a language with a lift in it, with a note of redemption from evil, of triumph over difficulties. It is the purest language spoken on this earth. And it is not confined to any one group or denomination. Anywhere the heart is open to Christ in simple surrender and obedience, it works. And it works with an almost mathematical precision. If collective verification has been tried and found workable, this is it.

This gives universal backing to our conviction. In Christ we have fact, not fancy. In Christian consciousness, we have our roots in the experiential – faith in Christ speaks certainty to the very depths. In the Christian Church, we have our roots in the collective – verification of my personal experience as evidenced in the lives of others. This lets me know that I am not off the track. This is it. All these coming together give me what I need – total backing.

The fifth and last step in the process of scientific verification is *a humble sharing of verified results*. Every scientist, when once he has verified the results of an experiment, proceeds to share those results with everyone who cares to listen. When once a Christian experiences the reality of Christ's transforming power at work in his heart, he then sets about the task of sharing it with as many as will listen. How could it be otherwise? A boy of 23, dying in a hospital, said to his pastor, 'Everybody has been so good to me. I haven't a thing in

2 Corinthians
3

the world to leave anybody. Couldn't I leave my eyes to somebody?' He offered his all – and he was happy in the offering.

Each one of us propagates something – whether we realise it or not. When we meet men and women, they give us a dominant impression – an impression of inner conflict or an impression of serenity and poise. The dominant impression we must leave with people is one of faith – not faith in our own faith but faith in His faith. We have seen that in today's scientific climate, many are concerned that their faith will not develop. But this is simply not true. When we allow the Divine Eagle to nudge us out of the nest, we may feel, when faced with the biting challenge of today's society, that our faith will fail us. But such will not be the case. Confronted with a challenge, a troubled faith has the very opportunity it needs to become a triumphant faith.

2 Corinthians 4:1–15

SOAR AWAY FROM ... PLAYING GAMES

Another reason why the Divine Eagle nudges us out of
the nest is because He *wants us to grow up and deal with
life realistically rather than defensively*. Many of us,
although we are adults, still behave like children. Our
outward behaviour, of course, is more sophisticated, but
inwardly we carry the same attitudes to life that we had
when we were growing up. One modern writer, Eric
Berne, has written a book entitled, *Games People Play*,
in which he shows that many of us go through life
playing childish games with each other. The word
'game' here is not to be understood as similar to
'Monopoly' or 'Snakes and Ladders', but as an attitude
we adopt when relating to other people, in which we
become defensive rather than honest.

Paul wrote to the Corinthian church about putting
away childish things. The Greek word used here is a very
forceful one – *Katageo* – which means to cut off, render
inoperative, disassociate from. Paul came to a place in
his life where he realised he was acting childishly and
needed to decide to stop acting that way – and grow up.
He did – and so must you.

1 Corinthians
13:1–13

A game is a device we use in our relationships with
God or others to stay at a childish level and thus opt out
of the responsibility of growing up. Many Bible characters
played such games. Take Moses, for example. The
children of Israel had been in bondage for hundreds of
years. Their wills were weakening. The stomachs of the
children swelled from hunger and the women cried for
deliverance. In the midst of their groanings, God heard
their request and chose a leader who was to be their
deliverer. But when God approached Moses at the

Exodus 4:1-17

burning bush, announced to him that He had confidence in him and would give him His support, Moses began to play one of the most repeated games in history. It is called, 'Yes ... but'. God would never have approached Moses and given him this great commission if He didn't believe him to be capable of it, but Moses reverted to the game that many of us play when confronted by reality.

We say, 'Yes, Lord, I hear what you say … *but* I'm not really capable … I'm afraid … and I have this problem or that problem … and so on.' The game is that we attempt to discount ourselves in the hope that God will pass over us. We are so afraid of failure, so entrenched in our own negative beliefs, so committed to self-humiliation, that we fail to see that God always equips when He calls. Do you play such games with God? If so then it's time to grow up. God wants to relate to you on a more adult level. He has tasks for you to perform, responsibilities for you to face. Decide to 'katargeo' (disconnect) your childish attitudes – now.

1 Corinthians 13:13
Genesis 3:1–12

The game Adam played is the first game of its type ever recorded in history. After eating the forbidden fruit, he would doubtless have felt the immediate effect of his sin in every part of his personality. One writer, in describing the effects of that original sin, says, 'Adam's body would have reeled, his legs fighting hard to support him. His brain would burn with fear and disbelief. Was this really happening to him? It was a feeling he had never experienced before. He found himself crying out like a man drowning in a stormy sea: "The woman You gave me – she gave me from the tree and I ate."' Here Adam laid down the foundations of a game that people have played ever since. The game is: 'If it weren't for you …' Adam blamed God because he reasoned that if Eve had not been created for him, there would have been no temptation to eat of the forbidden fruit. Was it God's fault? Apparently Adam thought that it was.

v. 12

How many times have you done the same thing? Something happens to you and you immediately blame someone else, perhaps even God. Many of us excuse ourselves with such statements as, 'If God had given me

a different wife ... If only I had been born into a different
family ... If circumstances had been different then
things would have been much better.' If ... If ... If.

If this is a game you play then let me make one thing

clear – no one ever grows in the Christian life until they accept the responsibility for the decisions they make, stop blaming others for their predicament and face the present realistically – and not defensively.

Cain also indulged in 'Games People Play'. Although he undoubtedly knew that God must be approached by an offering taken from the animal kingdom, he decided to offer instead an offering selected from the vegetable kingdom. It was an incorrect offering and he knew his gift would be unacceptable. Cain discounted God's commands and also the offering of his brother. Here we see Cain initiate a game called 'Uproar' – a game where conflict is purposefully started to avoid intimacy. It happens when a non-Christian, feeling drawn toward God and His Kingdom, sets up some argument or point of conflict in an attempt to prevent himself reaching the place where he has to surrender to God.

Genesis 4:1–16

In the early days of my Christian life, I could never understand why it was that a person, when close to the Kingdom of God, would say something like this, 'Why does God allow suffering?' Or, 'Why did God create the devil?' I came to see that such questions (not all) were really an unconscious attempt to keep God out of their hearts. You see, when God comes close to a person, their inner life is greatly disturbed. It must inevitably be so for inbred sin must be repented of, confessed and put away. But this game is not only played by unbelievers, it is played by some Christians also. When God draws near to your heart, you can choose to open yourself or create an issue which avoids spiritual intimacy. Is this a game *you* sometimes play?

Who hasn't heard of Jonah? The story of his encounter with the big fish is probably the most well-known of all

Jonah 1:1–17

the Old Testament stories – even though critics deny its validity. Personally I find no difficulty in believing the literal account of the story, especially when Jesus validates its significance in His statement in Matthew 12:40, 'For as Jonah was in the great fish for three days and three nights, so I, the Messiah, shall be in the heart of the earth three days and three nights' (TLB). Jonah was no exception when it came to playing games. His game was, 'See if you can catch me.' A grown man makes himself a fugitive in his own mind, sinks into fear and despair and crawls into a dark corner of a ship to hide from the Lord.

Matthew 12:40

Jonah 1:3

We play this game whenever we are unsure of ourselves (or of God), and go out of our way to get others to prove their interest in us by constant attention and follow-up. It's similar to a game we all played in childhood entitled 'Hide and Seek'. What it amounts to is this – we say, albeit unconsciously, to those who fill up the circle of our relationships, 'If you love me then prove it by dogging my footsteps, putting aside your own interests and engaging in ways that show me you are not willing to give me up.' This is immaturity at its worst. Maturity recognises that the best way to be loved is to be the initiator, not the receiver. The rewards of loving are to be loved.

Another game is one which the experts in game analysis call 'Stupid'. Simon Peter played this game. Picture the scene with me. Peter, the big fisherman, strong, resolute, determined, firm in his declaration of love for Christ, denies all knowledge of the Master. Why? He had walked with the Master for three whole years, heard Him speak the most wonderful words, saw Him heal the sick, raise the dead, cleanse the lepers and work other amazing miracles. Yet when he is asked if he knows Jesus, his response is one of withdrawal. In other words, he plays stupid. Eric Berne claims that whenever we play games, it is always for a reward. What was Peter's reward? It was the reinforcement of his fear.

Luke 22
47–62

Why, I hear you ask, should the reinforcement of his fear be a reward? Well, the more deeply he believed that he was afraid, and the more he did to reinforce that fear, the easier it would be to excuse himself for his failure to stand up for Jesus when confronted. The final pay-off was to protect himself from harm and danger. A Christian schoolteacher told me recently that whilst he was at an educational conference, someone happened to remark that the Bible was a fable. The man then turned to the schoolteacher and said, 'What do you think?' He told me that his first impulse was to play stupid and say, 'I am not sure,' or 'I don't know.' He caught himself just about to play the game, but instead accepted the

challenge of the situation and responded with some positive comments. To play the game of *Stupid* may bring temporary benefits, but the dishonesty involved greatly upsets one's spiritual balance.

Now we must turn our attention away from Bible characters and focus it fully on ourselves. Although everyone plays games in life – both Christians and non-Christians – the favourite game we Christians play is this: 'Let God do it.' Let me illustrate. Some time ago a lady asked me if I would pray with her about the difficulty she was having in her relationships with people. She said she felt rejected, no one seemed interested in her, and the people in her church just ignored her. I asked her, 'What are you doing about your problems?' She said, 'Well, I pray every morning and evening about them.' I said, 'That's fine – but what else are you doing?' She looked at me in amazement and said, 'What else can I do? If I pray enough about it, and get others to pray along with me, then won't God make the people who reject me a little more friendly toward me?' There was nothing wrong with her praying, but really she was playing a game. It was this: 'Let God do it.' She wanted God to do what He had already done – give her the ability to relate, share and have fellowship with others. What she needed to work on was her own attitudes. Someone has said, 'To have friends – be friendly.' Fortunately she took the advice I gave her, worked on it and began to see some success. If we are to get up out of our nests, soar into the air and enjoy the freedom of being mature then we must be able to differentiate between what we should be doing ourselves and what God alone can do in our lives and circumstances.

John 2:5

SOAR ... TOGETHER

We come now to the last of the specific issues that I have
interpreted as God's gentle nudgings to get us out of our
safe and comfortable nests. 'The Holy Spirit,' said
someone, 'comes not only to comfort the afflicted, but to
afflict the comfortable.' Nowhere is the truth more
clearly illustrated than in the issue now before us – *the
need to get out of the nest of our staunch denominational attitudes and begin to demonstrate to a sceptical
world the truth of Christian unity.*

I recognise, of course, that in all parts of the Church
there is a swing away from denominationalism toward
our true unity in Christ – but there is still a long way to
go.

John 17:20–26

In the Early Church the gulf between Jew and Gentile
was a very wide one. Peter, being a strict Jew, had to
undergo a shaking of his nest before he was prepared to
launch out and minister to the Gentile congregation
gathered in the house of Cornelius. The shaking came in
a vision that God gave him concerning all manner of
four-footed beasts – beasts which a strict Jew would
regard as unfit for human consumption. When God said,
'Rise, Peter; kill, and eat,' the command helped to
shatter his bigotry, and from here on he rises above his
denominationalism to be the means in God's hands of
bringing the Holy Spirit to the Gentiles. Later when
Peter is questioned by the leaders of the Church in
Jerusalem as to why he went to a Gentile congregation,
he recounts the vision God gave him and tells what
happened when he began to speak to those assembled in
Cornelius's home: 'As I began to speak, the Holy Spirit
fell on them just as on us at the beginning ... If then God

Acts 10:1–48

gave the same gift to them as he gave to us ... who was I Acts 11:15, 17 that I could withstand God?' (Acts 11:15, 17, RSV).

The entire episode in the house of Cornelius was indeed a shattering one for the Early Church. It forced them to examine their attitudes, check their preconceived ideas and be open to change. The time has come for us to do something similar. We must examine our hearts and distinguish between principles and prejudices, between man-made traditions and unchanging truths of God. There is a great shaking going on at the moment in many churches and fellowships. May we emerge from it – as did Peter – with a new vision and a new task.

The next great step in Christendom is the demonstrating of Christian unity. In a world and an age seeking unity, we Christians have little moral authority unless we can demonstrate to unbelievers that despite our denominations we are 'all one in Christ Jesus'. This does not mean that we have to disband our denominations (although I confess I wish we would), but to show men and women everywhere that unity in Christ is our first and primary concern.

Ephesians 4:1–16

But, you ask, how can we come together unless we agree on everything? We do not make that a prerequisite of fellowship in a home. The home can be united in spite of differences in temperament and belief. The one thing

that binds us together is the fact that we are children of the same parents. So it is in the family of God. Let that suffice. The differences are needed so that they can become growing points. The music of the Hindus is based on melody and not on harmony as is Western music. A Hindu hearing some negro-spiritual singing said, 'What a pity they can't all sing the same tune!' Had they done so it wouldn't have been harmony. The very difference made for richness!

Someone has said, 'The measure of our maturity can be and is measured by the breadth and depth of our capacity for fellowship with other Christians. *We are as mature as our fellowships.*' So if we cannot fellowship with other Christians, even though they belong to other denominations, we reveal our immaturity. What then is the basis of Christian fellowship? One thing and one thing only. Everyone who belongs to Christ belongs to everyone else who belongs to Christ. The basis of our fellowship is not around this doctrine or that doctrine. It is around Christ.

When John said that the disciples had seen a man casting out devils in Christ's Name and they had forbidden him they were simply revealing their immaturity. They would probably have said in justification that they were concerned about protecting their movement from impurities, irregularities and such like, but actually they were trying to protect their own prestige. The Pharisees came all the way from Jerusalem on one occasion to see the awakening under Jesus, but all they would see was that the disciples of Jesus ate with unwashed hands (Matt. 15:2). The movements of Jesus swept past them and left them grand relics. The same can be seen today. The

Luke 9:46–56

Matthew 15:2

movement for unity created by the Holy Spirit is sweeping across the world. Many sit clinging to a mode of baptism, a line of succession, an interpretation of doctrine and many other things. They let unity sweep right past them and they finish up – high and dry.

Although many are committed in theory to fellowship with all those who are truly committed to Christ and who belong to Him by faith, they find it difficult when it comes down to the actual reality of fellowship with certain individuals. They make such excuses as this: 'That person makes me uncomfortable.' Or, 'I can't seem to relate to that person as well as I am able to relate to others.' How do we overcome these difficulties? Perhaps in two ways: firstly, by saying to yourself, 'This is a person for whom Christ died. Christ loves him, and by absorbing Christ's love, so can I.' Meditate upon that fact until it filters through into your personality for, remember, what you think will soon affect the way you feel. Secondly, ask yourself, 'Why does this person act in this way? I will try to understand.' Then project yourself

Galatians
3:26–27

in to that person's situation and try to see life from their point of view. The capacity to project yourself into another person's situation will be the measure of your maturity.

When someone asked a famous businessman for the chief characteristic of an executive, he said, 'The willingness and the ability to project oneself into another person's situation, and to see things from his point of view.' If you come across someone with whom you constantly find it difficult to have fellowship, find out the reason, and if the reason is unreasonable, then dissolve it by your love. If the amount of love you give does not dissolve it, give more love and still more love. God fellowships with you not on the basis of you being worthy of that fellowship, but because of who He is. You

are to fellowship with everyone because of who you are – a lover of Christ.

We must understand the difference between disagreement and division. As Christians are we entitled to disagree with each other on matters of Biblical interpretation? Yes, of course, providing we disagree without being disagreeable. Christian unity does not mean that we have to agree on everything – we simply agree to disagree and go on loving each other as our Master commands us. Division, however, is another matter. This takes place when a person or a group of persons decides to take their disagreements further and exclude from fellowship those who do not share the same views. If it is true that when we belong to Christ, we belong to everyone else who belongs to Christ then such an action as this disrupts the unity of Christ's Body and wounds the heart of God.

Romans 16:17–20

Divisions come when people are more motivated by self-centredness, the itch for attention, the urge to be in the limelight, than they are by the proper functioning of Christ's Body. 'Watch out for those who cause divisions,' says the Scripture. We have a right to hold strong views of Scripture, but we must not let those views prevent us from sharing fellowship with those genuinely committed to Christ, but who may not see eye to eye with us. A letter I received said, 'What a pity that in *Revival* magazine you have a statement that says you believe in the infallibility of the Bible. This excludes millions of Catholics who believe in the infallibility of the Pope.' But it doesn't. There I stated what *I* believe. I do not make that a condition of fellowship. Interestingly enough in the same mail came an invitation to address a meeting in Westminster Cathedral!

v. 17

Let us look at the Jewish heart of Peter, obviously divided in its loyalty – wanting to keep Moses, representing the Law; Elijah, representing the Prophets; and Jesus, representing the new revelation, all on the same level. He said, 'Let us make three tabernacles.' This was serious, for the whole of the future was bound up with the question of whether Jesus was final, and whether supreme allegiance should be given to Him. It is significant that immediately following this statement, a cloud descended 'and they feared as they entered into the cloud'. Where there is division, there will always be clouds. No one would argue that there are clouds over our churches, and we fear as we enter those clouds.

Luke 9:28–36

Why are we afraid? The answer is simple – division. Each denomination is thinking in terms of itself, is losing a sense of the collective unity. But out of the cloud comes a Voice. God speaks! The voice is only of evaluation and invitation: 'This is my beloved Son: hear him.' The clouds will never lift and the fears will never depart until we listen to Christ. And what is He saying? This: 'That all of them may be one, Father, just as you are in me and I am in you ... that the world may believe that you have sent me'. Christ must come first, and the unity of His Body must take priority over any denominational allegiance. As the Divine Eagle nudges His Church toward the edge of the nest in an effort to cause it to soar above denominational divides, my prayer is that it will not be long now before we who share Christ's Name and nature, truly become *one*.

John 17:21